Forensic Crime Solvers

FINGERPRINT EVIDENCE

By Barbara B. Rollins
and Michael Dahl

Capstone
press

Mankato, Minnesota

Edge Books are published by Capstone Press
151 Good Counsel Drive, P.O. Box 669, Mankato, Minnesota 56002
http://www.capstonepress.com

Library of Congress Cataloging-in-Publication Data
Rollins, Barbara B.
   Fingerprint evidence / by Barbara B. Rollins and Michael Dahl.
   p. cm.—(Edge books, forensic crime solvers)
   Summary: Describes the types and features of fingerprints and discusses the
techniques used to take, develop, save, and compare fingerprints in order to solve crimes.
   Includes bibliographical references and index.
   ISBN 0-7368-2419-7 (hardcover)
   1. Fingerprints—Juvenile literature. 2. Criminal investigation—Juvenile literature.
[1. Fingerprints. 2. Criminal investigation.] I. Dahl, Michael. II. Title. III. Series.
HV6074.R62 2004
363.25'8—dc22   2003012703

Editorial Credits
Carrie Braulick, editor; Juliette Peters, series designer; Jo Miller, photo researcher

Photo Credits
AP/Wide World Photos, 22; Bill Cooke, 18; Keith Srakocic, 10
Barry Q. Cushman Photography, 15, 24
Brand X Pictures/William Fritsch, 6
Capstone Press/Gary Sundermeyer, 4, 8
Corbis, 25, 27, 29; Charles O'Reare, 16; Reuters NewMedia Inc., 7; SABA/Shepard
    Sherbell, 21
Folio Inc./Brown, cover; Pickerell, 20
Ingram Publishing, 28
Photo Researchers Inc./Mark C. Burnett, 1, 9; Science Photo Library, 14; Science
    Photo Library/Martin Dohrn, 12
South Carolina Criminal Justice Academy, 19
Tom Pantages, 13

**Capstone Press thanks David P. Peterson, latent print examiner at the
Minnesota Bureau of Criminal Apprehension, for his help in preparing
this book.**

1 2 3 4 5 6 09 08 07 06 05 04

Table of Contents

CHAPTER 1

Learn about:
- A murder scene
- Homicide detectives
- Crime scene investigators

The Body in the Kitchen

Apartment building owner Jim Stone walked toward Mariah's apartment. He planned to fix her sink. As he arrived, he saw the open front door. He peeked inside, hoping to see Mariah. Instead, he saw dark red spots on the kitchen floor.

Behind the counter, Jim found Mariah's body. He rushed to the telephone and punched in 911.

The Police Officers

The operator listened carefully to Jim. She typed information into her computer. Police officers near Mariah's apartment read the message on a screen in their patrol car. They turned on their car's siren, flashed the lights, and sped to the apartment.

A crime scene can leave
◄ important clues for investigators.

At the apartment, the officers checked to see if Mariah was still alive. They guessed she had been dead almost a day. They stretched yellow tape across the door. The tape kept people from entering the apartment.

Starting the Investigation

The homicide detective arrived. He saw blood on the walls. He also noticed overturned kitchen chairs. A rug was shoved out of place. He thought Mariah had fought with her killer.

Two crime scene investigators (CSIs) gathered evidence. The CSIs took photos of the body and the apartment. They collected blood from the floor tiles. They brushed powder on surfaces to find fingerprints. The powder

Police officers use yellow tape to prevent people from disturbing a crime scene.

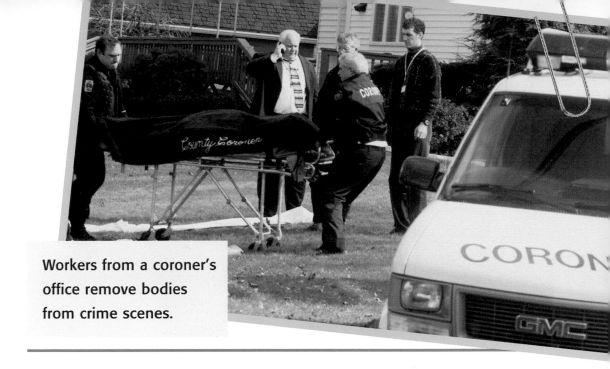

Workers from a coroner's office remove bodies from crime scenes.

showed a fingerprint on the kitchen table. The CSIs lifted the print with tape and placed it on a fingerprint card. On a cabinet door, they saw a bloody print shaped like an ear. They removed the door for evidence.

More police officers arrived. Some officers questioned Mariah's neighbors. Other officers talked with Jim.

Later, workers from the coroner's office arrived. They took Mariah's body from the apartment.

Detectives take notes to help them study crime scenes.

Important Evidence

The homicide detective thought about what he knew. Mariah lived alone. Her apartment locks were not damaged. Mariah's neighbors had not noticed strangers nearby. The detective needed more clues. He believed the best clues would come from fingerprints.

The detective entered the fingerprint from the kitchen table into a computer system. The computer compared it to other prints in the system. It showed similar prints on the screen. A fingerprint examiner studied the prints. The crime scene print matched the print of a man who had once been arrested for robbery. The detective learned the man lived in the area and worked as a pizza deliveryman. The police asked the man to come to the station.

At the police station, the detective asked the man if an impression could be taken of his ear. The man agreed. CSIs put lotion on his ear. They pressed a piece of glass against it. The CSIs dusted the ear print with powder and lifted it with tape. The ear impression matched the bloody ear print found on Mariah's kitchen cabinet.

Later, the man confessed to the crime. He had seen Mariah's money box when he delivered a pizza to her apartment. He tried to steal the box. He killed Mariah after she tried to stop him. The police arrested him for Mariah's murder.

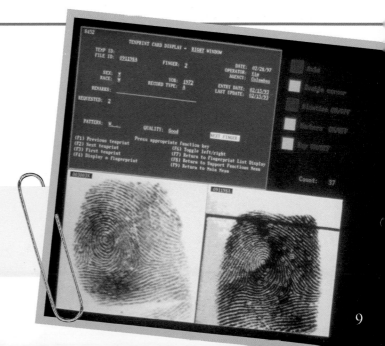

Fingerprint examiners can use computers to search for fingerprint matches.

CHAPTER 2

Learn about:

- Friction ridge skin
- How fingers leave prints
- Types of fingerprints

Fingerprint Features

Fingerprints are part of everyday surroundings. They are on drinking glasses, computer screens, paper, doors, and millions of other objects. Most people do not notice them. But fingerprints are important to crime investigators. Just one fingerprint can solve a case.

Friction Ridge Skin

The skin on the palms and inside fingers of a person's hands is covered with a swirling pattern of ridges. This friction ridge skin helps hands grip objects. The ridges curve, loop, and split to form patterns.

Each person has a different ridge skin pattern. Not even identical twins have the same pattern. Friction ridge skin patterns remain the same throughout a person's life.

Computer data can help fingerprint
◀ examiners study print features.

Patterns are on each person's fingers.

Fingerprints show friction ridge skin patterns. Body sweat and oil stick to the raised ridges. The sweat and oil is then left behind on objects that people touch.

Ridge Skin Patterns

The three main types of friction ridge skin patterns are arches, loops, and whorls. An arch can be plain or tented. A plain arch looks like an upside-down *U*. A tented arch looks like an upside-down *V*. In a loop pattern, the ridges enter at one side, curve, and come back to the same side. A whorl is a spiral or circular pattern.

Whorls can have pockets or double loops. A pocket is a small circle of ridges at the center of a whorl. Two whorls that meet in the center form a double loop.

Minutiae

Details of a fingerprint are called minutiae. Each print has several minutiae. A place where a ridge starts or stops is called an end. A place where a ridge divides is called a bifurcation. Ridges that split and come back together are called enclosures or islands.

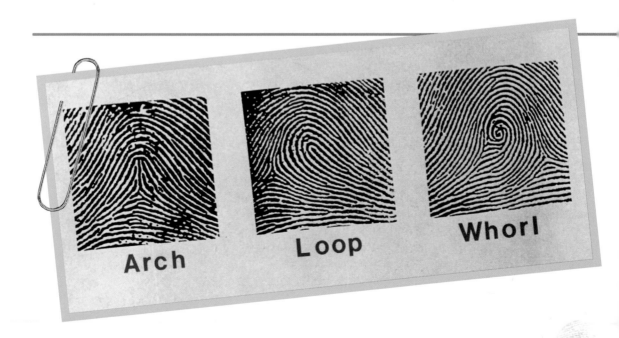

Arch   Loop   Whorl

The History of Fingerprinting

In the 1800s, interest in using fingerprints for identification grew. In the late 1850s, William Herschel was working as a government official in India. He required people to use their fingerprints to sign contracts. In 1880, English doctor Henry Faulds wrote an article about fingerprints. The article advanced the study of fingerprints for criminal investigations. Scientists Francis Galton and Sir Edward Henry classified fingerprint patterns. In the 1890s, law enforcement workers began arresting suspects based on fingerprint evidence.

In 1892, a woman from Argentina was found guilty of murder based on fingerprint evidence. During the next several years, fingerprint evidence became widely accepted as a way to identify suspects of crimes.

William
Herschel

Types of Fingerprints

Fingerprints can be one of several types. They can be patent, plastic, or latent. People can see patent prints without chemicals or equipment. Fingers dirty with blood, ink, or paint leave patent prints. Sweat and oil can leave patent prints on glass or metal surfaces.

Plastic fingerprints are molded into soft surfaces. These fingerprints may be in soap, wet cement, or wax.

Latent prints must be developed before they can be seen on surfaces. CSIs use chemicals and other supplies to see these prints.

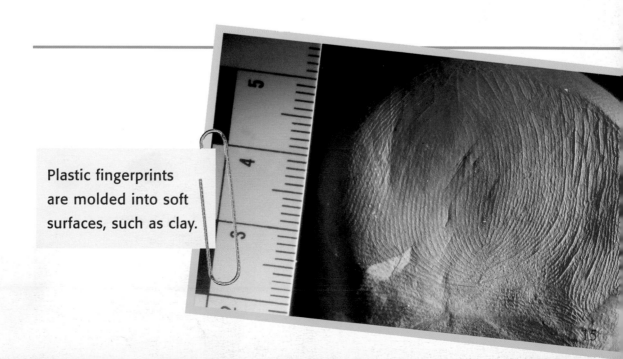

Plastic fingerprints are molded into soft surfaces, such as clay.

CHAPTER 3

Learn about:

- Ninhydrin
- Vacuum metal deposition
- Photographing fingerprints

Fingerprints at Work

Investigators can spend hours collecting fingerprint evidence at a crime scene. They photograph, develop, and save the fingerprints they find.

Developing Latent Prints

CSIs can make latent prints visible in several ways. They use lasers, filtered arc lamps, and other strong light sources. Light sources are least likely to harm fingerprints.

CSIs may use substances to develop prints. Heated superglue gives off fumes that make prints visible. A substance called ninhydrin is useful on paper, cardboard, and other surfaces that easily absorb water. Prints more than 50 years old have been developed with ninhydrin.

Lasers can help investigators
◀ see fingerprints.

CSIs sometimes dust metal powder on surfaces to develop latent prints.

CSIs sometimes brush metal powder over objects to develop latent prints. The powder sticks to a fingerprint's oil and sweat.

CSIs can have difficulty developing latent prints on certain surfaces. Vacuum metal deposition (VMD) is useful for these surfaces. A machine places thin layers of gold and zinc on an object. The gold sticks to a fingerprint's oil. The zinc settles in the spaces between the ridges. Investigators then can see the pattern.

Saving Fingerprints

Fingerprints found at crime scenes must be saved as evidence. CSIs usually press tape over prints developed with metal powder. They then lift the tape and place it on a paper fingerprint card.

CSIs often photograph prints. They use strong light sources to make a fingerprint easier to see. CSIs then take a close-up photo of the print. Later, the photograph can be enlarged to show details.

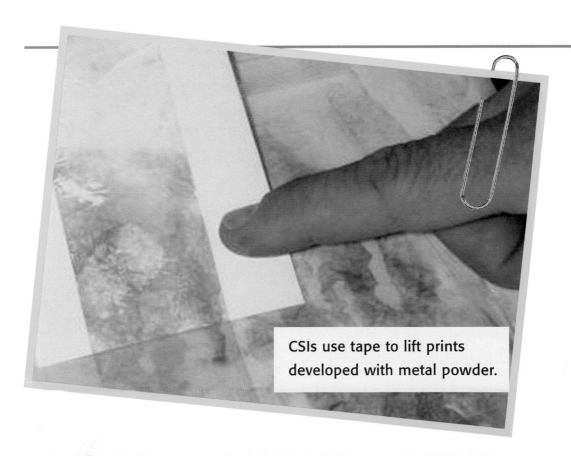

CSIs use tape to lift prints developed with metal powder.

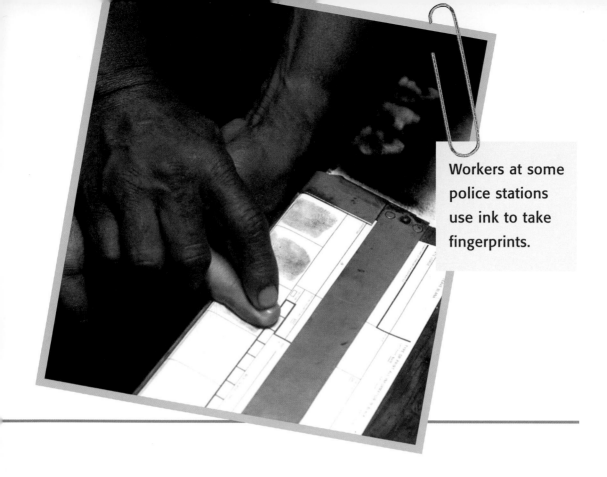

Workers at some police stations use ink to take fingerprints.

Taking Fingerprints

Investigators sometimes take fingerprints to help them sort out crime scene prints. They may take fingerprints of victims, victims' friends and family members, and suspects.

Some police stations use ink to take fingerprints. Workers first roll each finger in ink. They then press each finger onto a paper card. Electronic copies of the cards can be saved in computer databases.

Other police stations have an electronic fingerprinting system. A machine takes an electronic picture of fingerprints. These prints are stored in electronic databases.

Investigators sometimes need prints from dead bodies. After death, skin can become too dry for fingerprinting. Investigators soak the fingertips of bodies in chemicals to soften the skin. The fingertips are sometimes left in chemicals for weeks before they can be printed.

Fingers of bodies that have been in water also can be difficult to print. Skin breaks down quickly in water. Workers may slip loose skin off fingers and wear it like a glove to take a print.

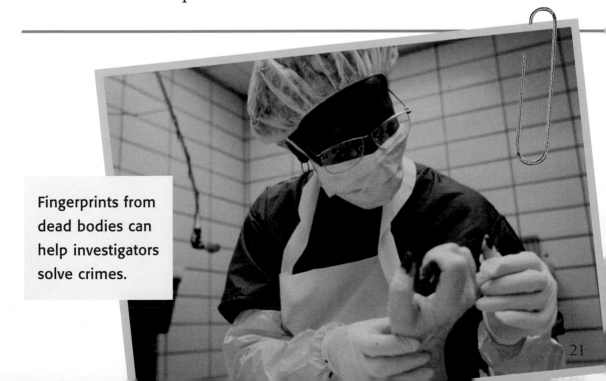

Fingerprints from dead bodies can help investigators solve crimes.

CHAPTER 4

Learn about:
- Comparing fingerprints
- IAFIS
- Using fingerprint evidence

The Evidence Fits Together

Fingerprint examiners compare crime scene prints to other prints on file. Some people with fingerprints on file have been arrested before. Other people have jobs that require fingerprints. Many of these people work for security companies.

Comparing Fingerprints

Fingerprint examiners look at many details when they compare prints. They look at a print's minutiae, ridge shapes, and ridge positions.

Examiners also search for matches in regional computer databases. Examiners enter the print into the system. The computer responds by showing a number of images. A fingerprint examiner must study the images to decide if a match has been made.

Fingerprint comparison can help
◀ investigators identify suspects.

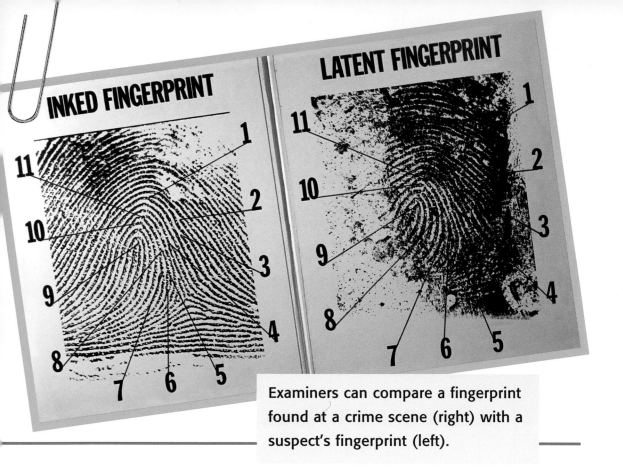

INKED FINGERPRINT

LATENT FINGERPRINT

Examiners can compare a fingerprint found at a crime scene (right) with a suspect's fingerprint (left).

IAFIS

Examiners sometimes do not find a match in their regional database. They then can search for a match in the Integrated Automated Fingerprint Identification System (IAFIS). The Federal Bureau of Investigation (FBI) runs this system.

The IAFIS can compare a print to more than 81 million fingerprint cards. Each day, the FBI enters about 40,000 new sets of prints into the computer system. Every second, IAFIS can compare 3,000 sets to find close matches. If none are found, the computer system saves the new print.

Besides matching fingerprints, the IAFIS provides criminal history information. This information can help investigators link crimes.

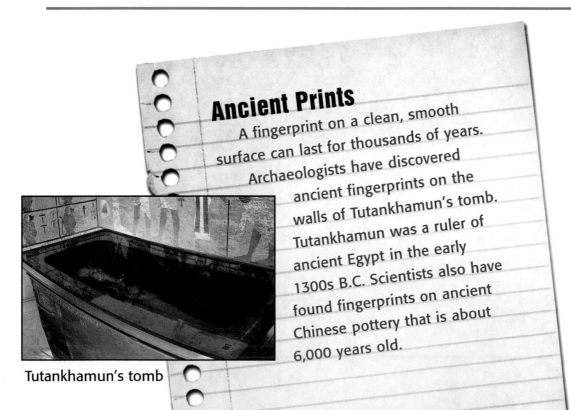

Ancient Prints

A fingerprint on a clean, smooth surface can last for thousands of years. Archaeologists have discovered ancient fingerprints on the walls of Tutankhamun's tomb. Tutankhamun was a ruler of ancient Egypt in the early 1300s B.C. Scientists also have found fingerprints on ancient Chinese pottery that is about 6,000 years old.

Tutankhamun's tomb

NCIC 2000

The IAFIS works with a system called the National Crime Information Center (NCIC) 2000. Through this system, police officers can scan the right index finger of a person they have pulled over. A computer identifies the friction ridge skin pattern of the finger. The computer system then compares it with fingerprints of wanted people in the United States.

Law enforcement officials can search the NCIC's database in two ways. They may do a search by looking for a match with only one fingerprint in the system. Officials may use this search if they believe they know the person's identity. A cold search tries to find a match with any print in the system.

Police officers can use the NCIC 2000 when they stop motorists. ➡

Fingerprints in the Courtroom

Many people have been found guilty of crimes based on fingerprint evidence. In 1911, Thomas Jennings became one of the first people found guilty of murder based on fingerprint evidence in the United States. Jennings was accused of breaking into the home of Clarence Hiller and his family. When Hiller saw Jennings, the two men fought. Hiller died after Jennings shot him during the fight. Police later found Jennings' fingerprints on a stair rail. The rail had been painted the night of the crime.

Fingerprint evidence is not always correct. In 1998, a Pennsylvania man was found guilty of murder based on fingerprint evidence. About two years later, he was freed after fingerprint examiners said an incorrect match had been made.

Fingerprints have helped investigators solve crimes for more than 100 years. Recent scientific advances have given investigators other forensic methods, but fingerprints are still one of the best forms of identification.

Fingerprint evidence is presented in many court cases in the United States.

Glossary

bifurcation (bye-fur-KAY-shuhn)—a place where a friction ridge divides

friction ridge skin (FRIK-shuhn RIJ SKIN)—a swirling pattern of lines on the skin of the hands and fingers; friction ridge skin helps hands grip objects.

fumes (FYOOMS)—gases, vapors, or smoke given off by chemicals

latent (LAY-tuhnt)—hidden from sight; latent fingerprints need to be developed to be seen.

minutia (muh-NOO-shuh)—a detail of a fingerprint pattern

patent (PAT-uhnt)—able to be seen with the naked eye; people can see patent fingerprints without developing them.

suspect (SUH-spekt)—someone thought to be responsible for a crime

Read More

Donkin, Andrew. *Crimebusters*. DK Readers. New York: Dorling Kindersley, 2001.

Parker, Janice. *Forgeries, Fingerprints, and Forensics: Crime*. Science at Work. Austin, Texas: Raintree Steck-Vaughn, 2000.

Pentland, Peter, and Pennie Stoyles. *Forensic Science*. Science and Scientists. Philadelphia: Chelsea House, 2003.

Woodford, Chris. *Criminal Investigation*. Science Fact Files. Austin, Texas: Raintree Steck-Vaughn, 2001.

Useful Addresses

Association of Certified Forensic Investigators of Canada
173 Homewood Avenue
Willowdale, ON M2M 1K4
Canada

National Center for Forensic Science
University of Central Florida
P.O. Box 162367
Orlando, FL 32816-2367

Internet Sites

FactHound offers a safe, fun way to find Internet sites related to this book. All of the sites on FactHound have been researched by our staff.

Here's how:

1. Visit *www.facthound.com*
2. Type in this special code **0736824197** for age-appropriate sites. Or enter a search word related to this book for a more general search.
3. Click on the Fetch It button.

FactHound will fetch the best sites for you!

Index